'Nasib Baik'

A Person of Good Fortune

By George Sandosham

This work depicts persons, events and memories in the life of the author as truthfully as recollection permits, and any opinions and portrayals are his own. Redhill Communications Pte Ltd makes no representation or warranties with respect to the accuracy or completeness of any information published, and will not be liable for any errors, omissions, or claims for loss of profit or other commercial damages, including but not limited to special, incidental, consequential or other damages arising out of use, inability to use, or with regards to the accuracy or sufficiency of the information contained in this work.

Cover and layout design by Redhill Studio, a division of Redhill Communications Pte Ltd.
Cover caricature of George Sandosham extracted from the Tanglin Club Gallery of Presidents,
Artist: The late James Ferrie

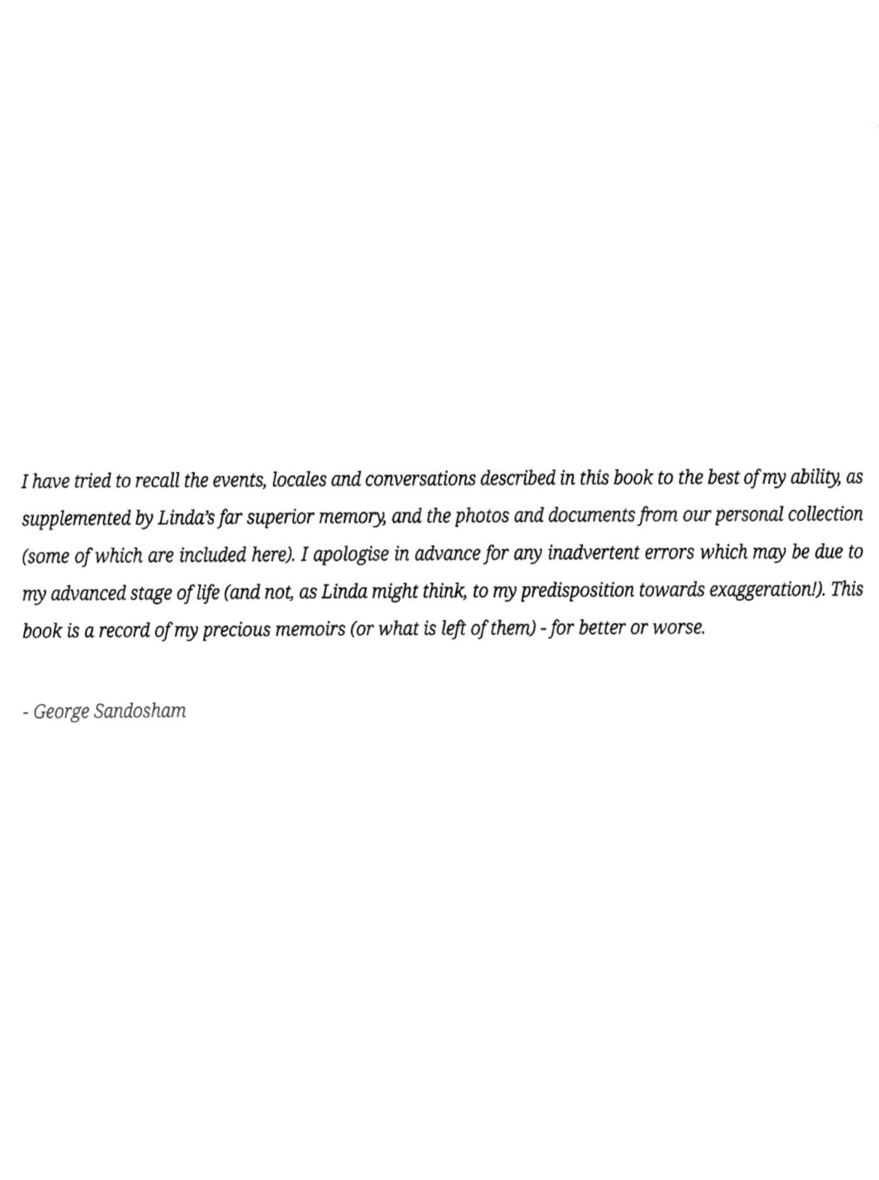

I have tried to recall the events, locales and conversations described in this book to the best of my ability, as supplemented by Linda's far superior memory, and the photos and documents from our personal collection (some of which are included here). I apologise in advance for any inadvertent errors which may be due to my advanced stage of life (and not, as Linda might think, to my predisposition towards exaggeration!). This book is a record of my precious memoirs (or what is left of them) - for better or worse.

- George Sandosham

"

Go, eat your food with gladness, and drink your wine with a joyful heart, for God has already approved what you do."

- Ecclesiastes 9:7 (New International Version (NIV) of the Holy Bible)

TABLE OF CONTENTS

1

FOREWORD

This short account of George Sandosham is both personal and partial – personal because George is my older brother by three years and you tend to have a particular view of someone close; and partial, because in 1964 I left Singapore to live in Australia when George was only 25. At the time, he was just embarking on his stellar legal career and this meant that we only met for short spells over the years on holidays. As such, I never really understood all the aspects of his working life, but I did catch glimpses of his busy social life, which was always fun.

What I hope to capture here as a foreword, are aspects of the 'essential' George that haven't changed even after many years and achieving fame and fortune. The 'George of good fortune' indeed, he was blessed with a very even temperament. I don't really remember him raising his voice in arguments (which he preferred to avoid) or having tantrums as a kid. I, on the other hand, was hot-tempered (christened 'chilli-padi' by our dad), and determined to win most arguments.

We were close in many ways, though he did resent my hero-worshipping of our elder brother, Reggie, who was nine years older. I met Reggie for the first time when George and I arrived in Singapore, having spent the war years in Kerala, South India. Reggie was nearly fifteen and spoke English, whilst I spoke Malayalam – could this stranger really be my brother, I wondered? I did learn English quickly, but when growing up, this difference in age and abilities gave Reggie a mystique in my eyes, which persisted for a very long time.

I was nasty and nice to George in equal measure, and that worked in reverse too, in his treatment of me. I was protective, and once – when he had a dispute with a boy in our neighbourhood who was closer to me in age – George asked if I could give this boy a punch. I did so without hesitation and the poor unsuspecting boy went home crying to his mother.

She subsequently arrived at our home, with the boy in tow, and complained to my father, who set up a 'kangaroo court' in his study and asked why I had punched Siva. I replied without hesitation, "because George asked me to". My father feigned seriousness and asked if I always did what George asked. I replied, "yes". He then asked, would I eat dog shit if George asked me to? That took the wind out of my sails.

Neither of us were brilliant students and the end-of-term signing of report cards was an issue. We would sometimes get my grandfather (who lived with us for some years) to attach his stamp with his signature. On a few occasions, I would ring Raffles Institution on the telephone and impersonate my mother. I spoke to the Cadet Master, the Sports Master or even the principal, claiming I was 'Mrs Sandosham' and could poor George be excused from cadets, sports, or exams because he was unwell.

I performed other minor 'duties' as George's sister – like ringing the houses of various girls whose parents would vet the speaker if it was a male. I also had to 'field' calls from some admiring females whom George had tired of! He was always particular with his appearance, sporting a crew cut when they first became popular in the 1950s, and a neighbour once described him as 'debonair'.

On one occasion, George helped himself to a present that had been given to me (a box of fine Swiss cotton handkerchiefs – the sort of present that was popular in the 1950s). He carefully separated them into two small piles of six items and gave one set to one girl and the other set to another girl that he was also keen on. Unfortunately, they were both in the same class at sixth form and boasted to each other that they had received a present from George!

This led to comparisons and revelations, but George's charm saw him through that minor catastrophe and he survived it. Charm is something he has lots of, and people of all ages were, and still are, willing to overlook minor misdemeanours of his.

In return for all my services, I was allowed to bask in George's fame as an athlete and good sportsman. There was the occasional downside to this – for instance, he asked me to walk on the other side of the road as we went to catch the bus to school, and not to talk to him on the bus as people would say to themselves, "What is a good-looking boy like him doing with a girl like that?" Fortunately, I have thick skin and took all slurs in my stride.

When growing up, Reggie and I felt somewhat superior to George. We thought of ourselves as 'intellectuals', interested in politics and ideas, whereas George was only interested in sports and food. He did say to me with a wry smile on one occasion, "I will be the only successful member of this family." After we had been in Australia for a few years and returned to Singapore for our first visit, we were met at the airport by his chauffeur driving a large Mercedes Benz. I thought to myself, how right he was!

There is no bitterness in George. He is generous in spirit and kind, and people are drawn into his orbit easily. He is witty but not malicious and doesn't hold grudges. Good things do happen to him. The best thing to happen to him is meeting his lovely wife Linda, his "child bride" as he likes to refer to her. The next best things are his lovely children and then his special sister!

I hope you enjoy reading this account of his life,

Sujatha Sandosham Pannell (George's sister)

2

PREFACE

Psalm 90, Verse 10 of the New International Version (NIV) of the Bible reads:

"Our days may come to seventy years,
or eighty, if our strength endures;
yet the best of them are but trouble and sorrow,
for they quickly pass, and we fly away."

Well, I am at the "quickly pass" and "fly away" stage, having surpassed eighty years of age. I was born in 1938, in the Year of the Tiger (which to me, explains my most committed pursuit and love of that certain local brew – Tiger beer). 1 February 2022 was the seventh Lunar New Year of the tiger in my life, and as I am of the view that the chances are slim that I will celebrate my eighth Lunar New Year in 2034 at 96 years old, I have decided to put my boring life into print, especially with the COVID-19 pandemic having confined me to my home for a while.

As far as I can remember, my mantra for success in life has been "as long as the beer is cold and the curry is hot, I am a content man". Yet long before I got to the legal drinking age, I still found my way to knowing how to make each day something worth enjoying. I attribute this a great deal to my parents, who, whilst determined individuals and champions in their own respective lives, raised us in a very 'easy-going' manner. We were allowed to be 'normal' human beings (I am comparing this to what I see happening to children these days in Singapore), and they never really imposed much on us.

This is the reason I have decided to name my book "A person of good fortune". It is not because I literally have a vast fortune in terms of dollars and cents, but because I have been blessed to have had a good and enjoyable life. The title is therefore a direct translation from the Malay term "nasib baik".

We once had a helper who lived with our family for 30 years – a Ms Ho Ah Eng (affectionately known as "Ah Soh" by all my friends). In the mid-1960s, Ah Soh helped Linda and I do virtually everything from housekeeping and looking after the kids to cooking, gardening and anything else she fancied. She used to call me "nasib baik" almost as a daily greeting, and I did not know what it meant in those days, but forty years later I was told that in Malay it meant "luck good".

I can certainly say that I have indeed lived a good and 'lucky' life where each and every person that I have met, the places I have been, and the choices I have made have played an important part in my life.

From my parents and siblings to my wife and children, and finally my colleagues and friends, I am indeed fortunate to have lived up to my best version because of all these people. A book about me, then, is also precisely a book about all these people. They have all helped me live with my idiosyncratic ideals, loved me for my eccentricities, and always accepted me. I imagine my life not as chapters – but as pieces of a puzzle that fit perfectly when one looks back on them. Those who currently do not fit will certainly fit in the next decade!

Of course, my wife thinks I should thank God here too, but our relationship has never needed that kind of clarification as I have lived most of my life according to the Holy Bible's principles (some of which will appear as you read through this book).

For all of you who venture through reading about my less than exciting life – I hope you will, if nothing else, have at least a chuckle. That is all I wish to bring to your life, and perhaps a tall pint of beer on a Tuesday at the Tanglin Club. Come and join me!

Best regards,
George

My parents

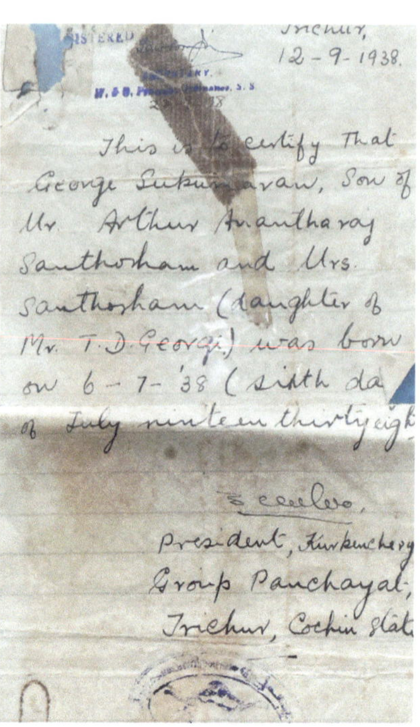

My birth certificate

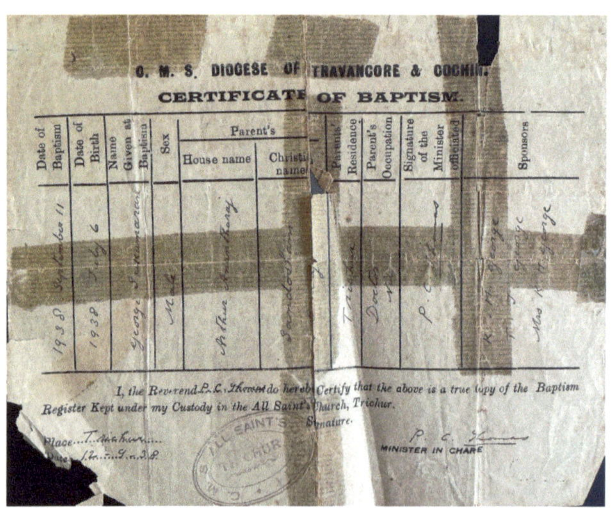

My certificate of baptism

George had humble beginnings.

But he grew up to be a man of many talents...

My charming demeanour no matter
the circumstance

My talent for food consumption

My early 'David Beckham' capabilities

3

MY EARLY YEARS

*The childhood events and memories which shaped my life from the
late 1930s to the early 1950s*

My first recollection of being alive, let alone of being a Sandosham, was when I was four years old. I recall it was in some 'wilderness' in India and remember, most vividly, a very strict grandfather on my mother's side who was the Chief Priest in the village church. His only preoccupation was to get me to church at least three times a day.

The next recollection I have was being sent to stay with an uncle (again, on my mother's side) in another part of the sub-continent. For some obscure, far-fetched reason, I seem to have lived in absolute fear of him and as such, looked forward to the monthly visits my mother made to see me. I have not the faintest idea why I should have feared him because when it was time for me to leave the beaches of Kerala at the ripe age of eight, I showed great reluctance to leave this kind uncle and his family.

My mother later informed me that the reason for my banishment was because I required discipline on account of my naughty and mischievous behaviour in my grandfather's house. This is a downright falsehood; I remember myself as always being a kind, well-behaved child, incapable of mischief.

My father, Arthur Anandraj (known as 'Sandy', short for 'Sandosham'), was born on the 9th of June, 1903 in Tamil Nadu, India. My mother, Emily George, was born in Trichur, Kerala. Dad graduated with a distinction in Medicine from the then-Raffles College in Singapore (founded in 1928, but later merged with the King Edward VII College of Medicine to form the University of Malaya in 1949). He got a job at the Medical Faculty, and on one trip back to Kerala for a visit, was introduced to my mother. A year after he graduated, my parents were engaged, then married.

My older brother Reggie was born in Singapore around 1933, and I followed after, the second son of my parents. Though I do not know why, I am told that Reggie lived with Dad in Singapore, whilst I continued to live in India with my mother. I have been told that during this time, Dad was spared the Japanese hostilities in Singapore as he was the head of the medical corps and was well versed in saving soldiers from malaria. He became an authority on the subject, as one of the few who knew how to treat and handle the tropical disease properly, and ended up writing a book and dedicating it to my mother.

Some photos I have show that we visited Singapore when I was young to see the other members of the family, and very soon after that, I ended up being the proverbial 'middle child' (with all of its syndromes) when my younger sister Sujatha was born in 1942. For her birth, my mother went back to India from Singapore as the Japanese hostilities in Singapore continued. I then stayed in India with my mother for the duration of this.

In 1946, we moved to Singapore to join Dad – it is here that I recall meeting the male members of my immediate family for the first time. I remember seeing Dad and my older brother at my aunt Mrs E. V. Davies' house, at the quarters which then fronted Bukit Timah Road. (It has now made way for a flyover and hawker centre.) We stayed with her for a while, and though I don't recall much more now – I knew that one of our neighbours at that time was none other than the High Court Judge (from 1978 to 1997) Mr S Sinnathuray.

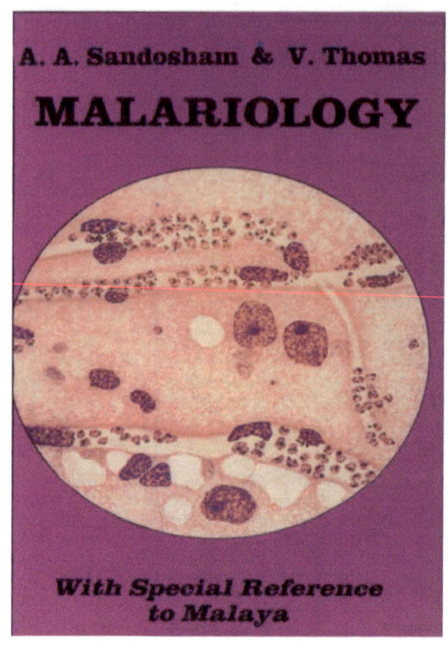

Book written by my father,
Dr Arthur Sandosham

The dedication of the book
to my mother, Emily

4

LIVING THE
SINGAPORE DREAM

My carefree childhood existence and my early sporting 'career'
in the 1940s to the 1950s

I was informed that when we first arrived in Singapore, I did not speak any known language except Malayalam, and was immediately enrolled in Pearls Hill School which is now People's Park.

At the age of eight, I was an overaged pupil, while the others were about six years old. I proceeded on the difficult task of mastering the English language and passing the exams, then getting admission into Outram Elementary School, which was next to the Old Prison at Pearl Bank. There, I partook in various sports activities and eventually became the champion athlete.

In my last year, I was honoured by being made a Head Prefect of the School. I was most thankful to the people who helped me a great deal, namely Mr Ponnusamy the Sports Master, Mr Ben Dudley the Principal, and Mr Norman D'Souza who painstakingly tutored me in Mathematics so that I could pass the exams.

During my earlier schooling days, I lived at No. 11 MacAlister Road, which consisted of quarters provided to the university staff and some of our neighbours included esteemed figures, such as the late Dr C J Oliveiro, Dr Lee Teow Seng, Dr Jansen (who was attached to the Dentistry department and was the Chairman of the National Cadet Corps), Dr Thamby Pillay, Dr Balasingam, and Dr Leong Peng Cheong.

We were fortunate to have a large field in front of the houses, where the younger members of our families spent most of the time playing games and various types of sports. Among the youngsters who became particularly prominent in the sporting field were Mr Balakrishnan, the son of Dr Balasingam who became captain of our national cricket team, and Dr Lindy Lin, who represented Singapore in badminton. Most of the heads of the families staying at MacAlister Road have since passed away.

We stayed at MacAlister Road from around 1947 to 1953 and then moved to No. 18 College Road when Dad was made Professor of Parasitology. It was a huge bungalow on top of a hill next to the Medical Faculty, and our neighbours were people like the late Professor Gordon Ransome, Professor E Monteiro who was the Vice-Chancellor of the University, and other leading lights.

I remember Dad having frequent, albeit friendly arguments, with his close friend, the late Dr B R Sreenivasan, on every aspect you could think of – you could tell when Dad was losing the argument as the volume of his voice used to go higher.

Given the house was located close to the King Edward College Hostel, I spent most of my time with the medical students there. I had many laughs with Prof A E Delilkan and could dedicate a chapter to his love life and courting days at the university leading up to his marriage to Prabha.

Another leading personality was Dr Lim Say Wan, with whom I partnered in badminton to win the University Doubles Title. Other close friends of mine were Dr Chan Onn Leng, Dr Raymond Lopes, and Dr Gopal Baratham, among many others.

It was an exciting and momentous time in Singapore during those years – not least because David Marshall had become the first Chief Minister of Singapore in 1955, but also because my parents gifted me my first car – a Fiat 600 – at the tender age of 16. To this day, it remains my sister's evidence that I was always the spoilt one in the family. Perhaps she is right.

After passing its entrance examinations, I was admitted to the great Raffles Institution (RI), which was then at Bras Basah Road (it is now a 70-storey City Hall mall and hotel). I entered RI when my elder brother Reggie had just left school to join the police force as a Probationary Inspector.

My first teacher was Mr Philip Liau, who subsequently became the Principal of the great school when it moved from the Bras Basah site to Grange Road. By sheer coincidence, Mr Liau ended up being my neighbour at Kingsmead Road.

One of my classmates was Mr Tan Cheng Guan, the second son of the late Justice Mr Tan Ah Tah, who in turn was the best man at Dad's wedding about 50 years ago. Mr Tan Cheng Guan subsequently went to Cambridge for his law degree and qualified as a Barrister.

At RI, we were encouraged to participate in all forms of sports activities. I played hockey and had the honour of being selected to represent the school during my first year in the 4 x 440 yards Inter-Malayan School Championships in Kuala Lumpur. We, however, only managed second place, being beaten by the Anglo-Chinese School (ACS) in Ipoh.

I excelled as a sportsman and in 1955, broke a long-jump record and was named the 'most promising athlete'. (If you look at me now, the only remaining physical 'evidence' of these achievements are some newspaper clippings and my son Rabi's equally accomplished abilities in track and field, which I somehow must have managed to pass down to him).

I spent most of the time on the sports field trying to pass all the examinations and after spending numerous hours on athletics, I had the distinction of being awarded the School Colours, which were presented to me by none other than the great Olympian, Jesse Owens. He was on a goodwill tour of the Far East and had been invited to present all the Sports Colours to the outstanding sportsmen in school.

I then managed to pass my School Certificate Examinations with sufficient points to be admitted to the Post School Certificate classes which are now known as Pre-University or Junior College. I recall that – of the 178 students who sat for the School Certificate Examinations that year – 176 passed the exams, and 91 of those received a Grade One. It was a remarkable performance and I was later informed that I had been accepted into the Law Faculty at the University of Singapore.

I can assure you that Dad, who was then the Principal of the University, had nothing to do with my being enrolled. I managed to get top-level passes in all the subjects attempted at Higher School Certificate (HSC) and most people found it hard to believe this, considering that I was one of the laziest pupils in the school.

Many of my colleagues at RI have been prominent citizens, holding high posts in the private and the public sectors. For example, there is Professor Tommy Koh, the Rector of Tembusu College and Ambassador-at-Large at Singapore's Ministry of Foreign Affairs (holding other prominent and public concurrent positions), and the late Mr Hwang Peng Yuan, former Vice Chairman of the Singapore Community Chest, amongst many others.

1959 was once again a momentous year for Singapore as on 30 May, the People's Action Party (PAP) won 43 of 51 seats and Lee Kuan Yew became the first Prime Minister. Encik bin Yusof Ishak became the Yang di-Pertuan Negara, Zubir Said presented the national anthem Majulah Singapura on 3 December, and I passed the Higher School Certificate examinations that year.

Luck was obviously with me again.

Sujatha and I, with the infamous car

My family

Caught in action in a long jump

My sprinting capabilities (above) were
shared by my son Rabi (below)

"

So I commend the enjoyment
of life, because there is nothing
better for a person under the
sun than to eat and drink
and be glad. Then joy will
accompany them in their toil
all the days of the life God has
given them under the sun."

- Ecclesiastes 8:15 (NIV)

5

LAW SCHOOL AND UNIVERSITY LIFE

How I came to choose Law as my career and make the most of Singapore's transformative years from the 1950s to the 1960s

As mentioned, my parents' style of parenting perhaps accounts for much of why Ah Soh called me 'nasib baik', and what has been described as my 'happy go-lucky' attitude. My siblings and I had very few restrictions or expectations; at the same time, our parents always provided for whatever we needed.

The only thing they might have expected of us was for us to go to university – but I always wanted to do that anyway as it was becoming apparent in Singapore at the time that if you did not have a degree, you were, in a way, a 'second class' citizen. (The education system was at the time being revamped to train a skilled workforce and this may have had an impact.)

Hence, I had the choice of a medical, engineering, or law degree. My parents did not impose on us to study things we did not find interesting or were not good at, so as none of the options caught my attention, I ultimately chose Law. This was not because it was some great passion I felt, but because when the time came to decide what to pursue, it was (in my view) the least difficult of the three.

Law was a popular course at the time because it was still relatively new – Chan Sek Keong and Tommy Koh were the first batch to graduate, and I would be the fourth. That is how I began my university journey as a young, passionate, and fun guy, enrolling at the National University of Singapore's four-year law degree programme in 1960 (five years for me).

I was then bundled off to stay at the Raffles Hall as I thought my parents had had enough of me living off and with them. The master of the hall was Mr Hon Yun Sen, whose brother was then the Minister of Finance in Singapore. The fellows who had the onerous task of keeping control over nearly 250 of us were Professor Kernail Singh Sandhu, Professor Arthur Rajaratnam, and subsequently, Mr Tan Eng Liang, who was the former Minister of State for National Development.

My first roommate at Raffles Hall was none other than Mr Edward D'Souza. He ended up being a colleague in the firm I started, having qualified as a Barrister. After being roommates twenty years ago, we still ended up 'roommates', in a manner of speaking. It was about this time that my mother was invited to be the honorary fellow at Eusoff College, the residential college for female students of the university. She later took on the role of Principal and was provided accommodation. Lucky for me, as Raffles Hall was only a stone's throw away, I had every excuse to visit the ladies' college on the pretext of visiting my mother!

As it turned out, studying law was easy – but having fun was easier! I continued my love affair with sports (having previously represented the university) and just had a good time at college. So, on paper, whilst I might have failed a year in college, in reality, I decided to spend an extra year at college to cherish my youth and time there (Linda attributes this to my chasing of girls but I cannot honestly pinpoint this as the sole reason, given there were a variety of interesting pursuits for me).

I made some great friends during those years, who went on to become district magistrates and political leaders in the coming decades. I can say, in hindsight, that having lived through some of Singapore's most historical periods, university life was fertile ground then for student politics and opinions to thrive within an engaging academic climate. Much to my dismay, this does not seem to be the case anymore.

This climate was not without controversy, however, and Dad was involved in some of this. He was the Vice-Chancellor of the University from 1959 to 1960 and Lee Kuan Yew had just become Prime Minister. There was fear of the communist influence, which made the political climate very sensitive and inconducive for the expression of alternative views.

Dad stepped down to oppose a civil service-wide policy requiring all civil servants (including lecturers) to take a 10 percent salary cut. University lecturers from overseas (including Dad) were not willing to accept this. This was interpreted as them 'being difficult' and funding was subsequently cut off from the university.

He eventually took up a position with the World Health Organization for malaria disease eradication in the Philippines and later became the head of the Institute of Medical Research in Kuala Lumpur. At one point, he was publicly accused of being a 'deserter' because he left Singapore. I wrote to the newspapers to defend him, considering this to be part of my God-given duty as his son[1].

In truth, my parents continued with their so called 'good works' all their lives, and I include this photo here of the 'Sandosham Home' in Trichur, India - a home for the elderly which they founded. My mother always had this idea to start a retirement home in Singapore, but as the Asian custom is for most elderly persons to reside with their family, the idea never really took flight. However, when my parents went back to India, they ended up building such a home.

At the time, many Indians were working overseas and couldn't care for their elderly parents back home. There was a need to have them well cared for and attended to. Sandosham House provides just this care for them, assuring much peace of mind for those abroad. In fact, many of my father's old students and his colleagues in Singapore contributed the funds to build the home. Such was their legacy as contributed to by the life they had built in Singapore and close ties they had made.

Life at university was more than a simple rite of passage in those days – that period was some of the most turbulent and transformative times for Singapore, and the restlessness of the nation was felt throughout our university life. We knew we were on the cusp of transformation. On 1 September 1962, Lee Kuan Yew called for a referendum on the merger with Malaysia. Nearly a year later, on 9 July 1963, he stood in front of a crowd at the Padang declaring Singapore's independence from the UK; finally, on 9 August 1965, he announced in a televised press conference that Singapore had become a sovereign, independent nation and that Yusof bin Ishak had been appointed as our first President.

---

[1] As mentioned in my prologue, although I am not overtly religious, I do believe in the Judeo-Christian God, and that if I do anything wrong, I will be punished. For instance, whilst at university, I woke up early and 'religiously' took the bus to St. Andrew's Cathedral to attend the services there, which started at 7:30 am. Nowadays I recite the Lord's Prayer six to eight times a day, which happily coincides with the number of times I feel the urge to relieve myself a day. (Linda does not approve of me blaspheming in this way but it is true that I am therefore reminded to say the prayer at these times.)

Sandosham Home, Trichur, Kerala

"

Enjoy life with your wife, whom you love, all the days of this meaningless life that God has given you under the sun—all your meaningless days. For this is your lot in life and in your toilsome labor under the sun."

6

MEETING LINDA, THE LOVE OF MY LIFE

My carefree life would not have been possible without the love of my wife,
who has seen me through (being) thick and thin

As it turned out, the relatively 'activist' and engaging climate at university, coupled with the evolution of Singapore as a nation during those days, formed the background for my meeting Linda. She was studying arts during the same years as I was at Law school but was far more involved and interested in student politics than I ever was.

For instance, we both found ourselves participating in the Professor Enright rallies which centered around defending the university's academic autonomy. As a foreign lecturer, Enright had expressed views about how the government was approaching the forging of a national identity. This was not looked kindly upon, especially at a time when the government was trying to clamp down on what it saw as the promulgation of Western values and ideals.

As I recall, a mutual close friend of ours was a leader of the student union, and participated in leading the demonstrations which Linda and I joined.

However, looking back now, I can hardly call my role that of a 'demonstrator', let alone think of the rally as a 'demonstration'. In truth, I probably found myself there because it seemed to be a grand social occasion I shouldn't miss – especially if there were going to be many passionate female students attending!

Perhaps the concern of the university and the reason that it was high profile were that it could have erupted along the lines of the Chinese Middle School riots which happened in June 1956. Lim Yew Hock had succeeded David Marshall as the Chief Minister of Singapore and initiated a series of arrests and banning of pro-communist groups, including the deregistration of the Singapore Chinese Middle Schools Students' Union (SCMSSU). The students responded by threatening a sit-in until the SCMSSU was reinstated.

In the end, nobody got into trouble, but these experiences, other university-centred activities and our common friends were what brought Linda and I closer together – and subsequently why we fell in love – though how we actually met remains a point of debate.

She seems to believe it otherwise, but I know that she first became attracted to me when she saw me at the track and field events. A lean and strong guy, beating all the other guys – of course, that is a sight to behold! As such, despite Law not being my first passion, I will always be glad I entered the faculty as otherwise, I would not have met Linda.

Once we began formally dating, I became aware of just how much of an impact my parents' easy-going attitude in raising us had made on our lives. It meant that not only were we allowed to choose what to study – we were also allowed to choose whoever we wanted to marry. I only later came to realise that this was, perhaps, highly unusual for the time.

My brother married Jane Vias, a Sikh lady, whilst my sister married an Englishman named Richard Pannell, an English Literature lecturer who later became a lecturer at Monash University in Melbourne, Australia. I of course ended up marrying Linda, who is of Chinese ethnicity, but none of this was at all an issue for our family.

In fact, my mother says that my marriage to Linda was somewhat prophesied at an early age given my disproportionate love of Chinese food from around the age of 10 (which she attributes to the fact that she could only stomach congee when she was pregnant with me). The irony is that Linda now cooks Indian food more often than not!

Linda, for her part, has always spoken her mind without fear and continues to do so to this day – something that I deeply admire about her. At that time, Singapore was young, as were we, and we all had a long and promising life ahead.

Linda at graduation

7

LIFE IN THE SINGAPORE LEGAL SERVICE

How I survived the start of my legal career in the mid-1960s

After much blood, sweat, and tears, I finally graduated with a Law Degree in 1965, the same year as Singapore's independence. I even managed to surprise my parents by not only passing the examinations but getting a Class 2 Honours Degree and being placed third in order of merit in my class of 78 students in the final year.

Dad was so delighted by my performance that he gave me S$1,000 in cash, which I promptly spent on him at the Bukit Bintang Cabaret in KL as my mother was away in Australia.

However, the biggest shock to my family was when I was accepted by the Law Faculty to be a Graduate Assistant, giving tutorials to first-year students, as the faculty members felt that I had academic capabilities like my father. How wrong they were.

Upon graduation, Mr Jayakumar, who later became a Professor in the Law Faculty, was instrumental in getting me a fellowship to attend the Academy of American and International Law at the Southern Methodist University in Dallas, Texas from June to July 1965.

I proceeded to Dallas immediately upon being conferred my degree at the Convocation. I flew non-stop (except for refuelling), which took about at least 24 hours, with several stops at Saigon, Manila, Guam, Wake Island, Hawaii and San Francisco. I then took a small Boeing 707 Pan Am flight (the airline no longer exists) to Dallas and swore after that experience never to fly again for more than an hour at a stretch.

In Dallas, the only contribution I made to the legal seminars was that I managed to outdrink all the delegates on the campus as well as all the footballers in the Dallas Cowboy Team while staying at the Lawyer's Inn. I subsequently went on a 'round the world' tour of sorts – I flew from Dallas to New York, then London and Calcutta. In Calcutta, I went to visit my ex-college roommate, Dr Raymond Lopes – he hadn't passed his medical degree in Singapore and had moved to Calcutta to complete this.

Calcutta formed a permanent and depressing impression on me – the poverty was harrowing, the people were living in such squalor on the streets, and children were walking around without any clothes and rummaging in bins for food. It is a sight I could never forget, and I swore at the time I would never return to India as I could never have imagined the pain and misery these people lived with. While I did make subsequent trips with Linda, the tragedy that follows poverty always shook me.

I then returned to Singapore and set about earning a living. I read in Chambers at Braddell Brothers under my master Mr P Coomarasamy, who subsequently became Singapore's Ambassador to Washington, D.C. I was then admitted to the Singapore Bar (to practice law) and as I decided I was not suited to be an academician, I embarked on my career of practice.

I applied for the legal service as all my friends were there (Mr N Ganesan, Mr S Rajendran, Mr Errol Foenander, and Mr Anwarul Haque in particular). It was also known as the 'iron rice bowl' because working for the government meant job security. I was selected after an interview by the Legal Service Commission which comprised the (then) Chief Justice Mr Wee Chong Jin, Attorney-General Encik Ahmad Ibrahim, Chairman of the Public Service Commission Mr Phay Seng Huat, and Justice Mr F A Chua.

My first posting was in 1966 – as a Magistrate at the Criminal District and the 8th Magistrate Court at South Bridge Road. It was near Hong Lim Green, opposite the old central police station. I was 26 years old, and the first District Judge and Magistrate at the time was Justice Mr Dennis D'Cotta (subsequently elevated to the High Court Bench).

Among my colleagues in the courts at the time were Mr N Ganesan, Chairman of the Football Association of Singapore, Mr Anwarul Haque, a brilliant international hockey goalkeeper, Mr S Rajendran, a senior partner at one of the legal firms in Singapore, and many others. One of the most respected members was Mr K T Alexander, who acted as a guide and mentor.

As a magistrate, I presided over many cases, but some that stand out include a motorist who told me he would rather go to jail than admit guilt (via a plea), my acquittal of a man who had an asthma attack whilst driving and was charged with allowing someone else to drive his car without third-party insurance, and finding guilty two men who went to great lengths in an elaborate scheme to repeatedly commit the crime of Outrage of Modesty on young women.

I was also assigned to listen to all the racial riot cases, which were the bane of Singapore at the time. As most of the cases involved Malay and Chinese people, they thought it best to have an Indian person presiding as a 'neutral' figure and so they picked me. There were so many accused persons that they had converted some of the school halls into courts to be able to accommodate everyone. At any one time, there were around 200 to 300 accused persons, and they were all charged.

I also happened to swear in the first batch of National Service (NS) men. In preparation for this, I had asked them to state "I (insert your name) swear allegiance...". The practice went well, but at the real ceremony the boys actually said the exact words "I, insert your name"!

By the way, this was 55 years ago. Now it is 2022 and I hear that our national servicemen are getting S$100. I want to know why I don't also get my money – plus interest!

By that time, Linda had left for Cameron Highlands in Pahang, Malaysia to teach and I remember writing letters to her. I had driven up all the way from Singapore to Cameron Highlands with my good friend Ram Naidu to satisfy my curiosity as to where Linda was living. Of course, it sufficed as a kind of joyride and mini holiday for us both too.

Not long after, Linda and I decided to marry and in truth, it was an easy decision. You see, as a legal service officer, I went to our office clerk one day to ask about the monthly salary, and the clerk said, "your basic pay is S$600, but you get a living allowance – S$150 if you are single, S$300 if you are married."

Well, needless to say, the decision was immediately made and after a long search which lasted all of three weeks, I decided to marry Linda (née Chiem Siew Leen) – and the rest, as they say, is history. (I say this mainly tongue in cheek because as many of you reading this will know, I owe my long-suffering wife a great deal, as the cartoon below indicates).

Extract from original comic strip 'Hagar the Horrible' by Chris Browne

My graduation

District Judges and Magistrates – 1967

“

Marriage should be honored by all,
and the marriage bed kept pure,
for God will judge the adulterer
and all the sexually immoral.
Keep your lives free from the love
of money and be content with
what you have, because God has
said 'Never will I leave you; never
will I forsake you.'"

– Hebrews 13:4-5

8

OUR WEDDING AND SILVER ANNIVERSARY

The eventful day of 7 May 1966 and our 25th wedding anniversary celebrations

Our wedding was an unexpected adventure of its own. As I said, the decision to marry Linda was an easy one, but concurrently being part of the legal service made things a little trickier.

The day of our wedding was a Saturday, and I had a court case. I had anticipated that the defendant was going to plead guilty, so Linda and I had planned to get our marriage registered at the registry of marriages post-lunch. As luck or the defendant would have it, he decided to suddenly claim trial! Here I was happily planning to get a half-day off from work and get married, but the defendant had other plans.

As soon as I heard that, I rushed to my dear friend and colleague, Amarjit Singh, and asked him if he could take the case forward that day. "What's your excuse this time?", he jokingly asked. "I'm getting married!" I said. It took Amarjit a few seconds to realise that I was serious, and he kindly went ahead with my case. I got to the registry on time and Linda, thankfully, did not turn into a runaway bride.

The wedding was a quiet affair with just my folks and my wife's father, Dato Chiem, being present at the solemnisation. Her mother was too heartbroken to see her daughter going against her wishes to marry an Indian-origin fellow who, she felt, would not be able to look after her daughter.

Shortly after registering the marriage, for want of something better to do, we adjourned to the Turf Club to witness the races before the reception in the evening. I think it was a lucky day, not only because we were married but also because we ended up betting and winning! It was in the last race when my wife picked horses No. 1 and No. 11 to finish first and second. They did just that and it paid S$111.

What a coincidence! It just about paid for the reception for the small group we had that evening. I recall Mr P Coomaswamy, my Master in Chambers, advising me to ensure that my wife would allow me out at least once a week with the boys, but he said, "Don't waste it on the boys."

That was not the last time we went to the club, but definitely one of the most memorable outings. I would highly recommend splurging your betting wins on friends, especially those who volunteer to take your case in the middle of your wedding day.

Reggie and his wife, Jane, hosted our wedding reception at Reggie's place that evening. I remember we had over 30 people, but among them were our dear friends Dr Mulkit Singh, Dr Ung Eng Lim, Anwarul Haq, my best man Tong Yew Sum, Linda's bridesmaid Veronica Ung and her college roommate Doreen Thambiayah.

As far as weddings go, ours was regarded as a rather modest affair and as such, 25 years later when Linda and I celebrated our silver wedding anniversary, I decided on a bigger-scale celebration. After all, I had survived 25 years of 'penal servitude' with the same wife!

To be honest, my perception of 'bigger scale' only implies more friends, food and most importantly, beer. It would otherwise be as informal and friendly as any gathering of old mates. But lo and behold! The celebration turned out to be a more notable event than I had ever imagined – far from a mere afterthought of the quiet wedding 25 years ago!

What happened was that a few weeks before the celebration, (I was then President of the Tanglin Club), I hosted the then-President of Singapore Mr Wee Kim Wee and his wife at dinner to present him with his Tanglin Club membership. In the course of the conversation, I mentioned that I was celebrating my 25th wedding anniversary and casually and unwittingly invited him to join in the celebrations – fully expecting him to laugh it off.

Much to my shock, he said quite seriously he would need a formal invitation with all the necessary details sent to his office. Immediately thereafter began a great flurry of events which took place right to the day of the anniversary celebrations.

That same evening after the President and the First Lady left the club, I was badly in need of a beer to end the evening. By sheer coincidence, I had the pleasure of being introduced to the then-British High Commissioner Gordon Duggan and his wife Erica that night. The topic of our conversation was the invitation to our 25th wedding anniversary and as it turned out, the Duggans announced that they were married on 10 May. There was no way I could not also invite them to join in the celebration, which they happily did. You could say that our quiet and humble wedding ceremony was more than made up for at our silver anniversary 25 years later!

Our Silver Anniversary celebrations with
former President of Singapore Mr Wee Kim Wee in attendance

▲ *"Cutting the cake, May 7th 1966!"*
▼ *"25 years later..."*

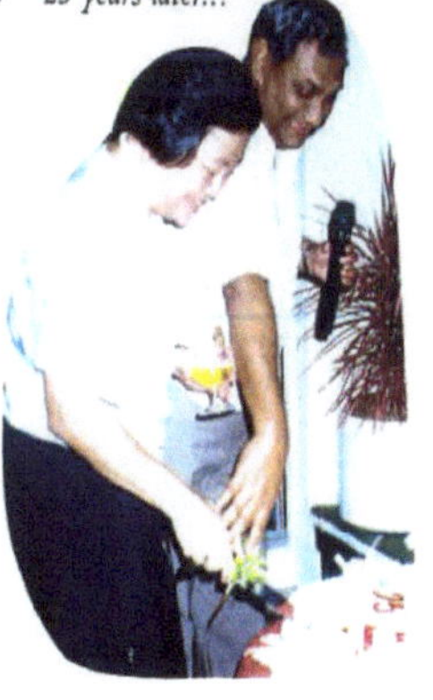

Thank You

As George Sandosham steps down from Presidency of the Club, and from the General Committee, it is timely to extend our thanks for his contribution over the years. George joined the Tanglin Club in 1971 and has served on the General Committee in various capacities since 1982. The tolerance of Linda, his wife, was also noted and appreciated at the AGM and they have been elected Life Members. We do hope George and Linda who have recently celebrated their silver wedding anniversary will forgive us for the following snippet of history:

A quote from his Mother reads: "I remember when George was a young boy he used to tell me that he will marry a Chinese girl as he was more fond of Chinese food than Indian!"

Extract from Tanglin Club magazine

9

PRIVATE PRACTICE

How I came to set up my law firm and life in private practice in the 1970s

In 1969, after three years of being a magistrate, I was promoted to be a Criminal District Judge. This essentially meant I had greater sentencing powers and could issue longer jail terms and more strokes of the cane for criminal transgressions.

After four years of this and being on the bench, I went on to become a Deputy Public Prosecutor (DPP) in 1970 and one of my bosses was Francis Seow, who was then promoted to be the Solicitor-General. Unfortunately, he later had a rather infamous clash with the government and ended up leaving for America.

At this point, I also decided to leave the legal service – though my reason was less controversial. I was not getting promoted, you see, and it was no secret that my beer-drinking activities at the Singapore Cricket Club were not exactly endorsed by the public prosecutor's office.

This skill did end up leading me to find my fortune, however. Because I was a member of so many clubs, I also met a lot of varied individuals who also happened to be wealthy. My skill, coupled with my very likeable character (after all, 'San-tho-sham' means 'happiness' in Sanskrit!), led to a Mr Horace Langlois, a gentleman I met at one of these clubs, offering to 'set me up' with an office and clients. In June 1971, I decided to take up his offer.

Initially, it was a one-man show. Over time, we had five lawyers – including my former college roommate Edward D'Souza (who subsequently did a Law degree after his Arts degree); Puvenendran, who used to be the Head of Homicide at the Criminal Investigations Department and who has unfortunately now passed away; Alan Thambiayah, who read in Chambers with me and is now a top arbitrator; Ram

Goswami, a very hardworking and quiet lawyer; and Gurdip Singh, who also read in Chambers with me and to whom I eventually ended up giving the firm to.

One of the first cases involved Isaac Paul Ratnam – a former colleague when I was a DPP. He approached me as he had gone to work for Francis Seow (who had left Singapore) and was charged with instigating the dishonest removal of property and causing evidence to disappear. Mr S Rajendran was prosecuting at the time, and Isaac pleaded guilty. I presented his mitigation plea before Senior District Judge Mr TS Sinnathurai to say he had acted out of stupidity and not criminal intent.

Another memorable one was with David Marshall, where we were both defending co-accused persons – my client was charged with rape and his client with attempted rape. I asked David, "What is his defence?" David said, "He's incapable of having an erection, in which case, he cannot 'attempt to rape'." However, I researched this and found an English case that said even if you are impotent, you can be guilty of an attempt. In mitigation, David said, "How can my client be charged when he's incapable of having sex?" And so, the judge agreed and acquitted his client!

Well, as they say – "the law can be an ass".

As defence counsel, I lost three guys to the gallows due to the discharge of a firearm, which carries a mandatory death sentence. They didn't even kill anyone, and two of them were not even present at the scene! However, as two of them knew the third guy had possession of the firearm and did nothing to stop him, they were convicted and sent to the gallows. They didn't even get to give evidence – the judge convicted them regardless as there was 'intent to cause injury'. I could not disprove this because my client shot the bullet and it had lodged just within an inch of the victim's neck.

However, I did save one guy from a certain death sentence on a last-minute technicality. My client was charged together with four other persons, as well as a 'person unknown' for murder. All of them testified that someone took a knife and stabbed the victim to death but three of them were below 19 years old, so they couldn't be hanged. However, my client was 21 years old, so could be hanged.

I asked the judges – Justices Punch Coomarasamy and S. Rajandran – "the charge says 'my client and four others and unknown' stabbed so and so to death – do you know who this unknown person is?" The investigating officer (IO) said, "we know". Then the judges asked, "Then why isn't he in the charge?" The IO said, "We only recently arrested him".

Then I asked, "do you have him in custody?" They said "yes" – so I said this unknown person would have been a witness, and I wanted to call him. They let me call him as a witness, and I said, "I only have one question – did my client stab the accused?" He said "no" – so the judges didn't know what to do.

Through that, I negotiated the charge down to culpable homicide – which is a reduced charge from murder, and my client avoided the gallows.

In another rather novel drugs case – I defended one guy who was caught coming across from the causeway with 1kg of heroin. He had been framed, and I managed to prove it because of a simple piece of evidence – a mere receipt! It proved he had been set up and he only got a few years in jail instead of being charged with trafficking – which is a capital offence.

Some of my cases were rather spirited during proceedings and reported in the press as such, with a few fortunate wins including getting a bigamy charge withdrawn, having a jail term set aside to give the youth another chance, having a charge amended due to unclear evidence, and getting a caning sentence withdrawn for a client who was medically unfit. I also somehow managed to successfully argue on one matter that a District Judge had exceeded sentencing powers, and proposed separately at a different trial that sentencing should be uniform for the same types of cases.

I also did a few cases pro bono and served as the Chair of the Criminal Law Advisory Committee for 12 years. I was awarded a public service award (known as the 'Pingat

Bakti Masyarakat' (PBM) in Singapore) in 1986 for my work with persons detained without trial, seeing through their representations, and making a legal analysis and recommendation as to the next steps.

The PBM is a Singaporean national honour that was instituted in 1973 – awarded to any person who has rendered commendable public service in Singapore or for his or her achievements. Given detention was a twice-yearly affair and I am bound by the Official Secrets Act, the only material information I can divulge about being awarded the PBM is that I celebrated by being 'Pissed By Midnight'!

That same year, Linda also won the Efficiency Medal (Pingat Berkerbolehan) for her work at the Ministry of Education the same year as I did for her contributions to the education sector and when we both learned that the other had also gotten a medal – we teased each other about whose award was 'better'. The Straits Times even published that!

On 1st March 1994, I was appointed as a Justice of the Peace, a position which is appointed by the President of Singapore. Ong Teng Cheong officiated our ceremony. At the time, the functions, powers and duties of a Justice of Peace ranged from being able to officiate weddings, laying a complaint under the Children and Young Persons Act, and issuing a search warrant under the Official Secrets Act, to examining ships in distress and enabling statutory declarations.

Of all these duties, I was particularly interested in the Visiting Justice, under the Prisons Act. We could inspect the wards, cells, yards, and solitary confinement cells, test the quality and quantity of prison food, as well as hear prisoner complaints.

Once, I visited Changi Prison and I remember asking the prisoners if everything was okay. One prisoner asked for my help to get his glasses back from the warden so that he could read books. I asked the warden about that, and he told me that his glasses were taken away due to them being made of pure glass and that they were deemed to be an unsafe item and potential weapon.

In 1994, as I was preparing for retirement, I ended up giving the private practice firm to my colleague Mr Gurdip Singh, who I mentioned earlier. He was a former police prosecutor who then qualified as a lawyer. The firm is now called 'Gurdip and Gill'.

Photo of my namecard at my firm

Photo of Horace and I

Photo with my private
practice colleagues

Photo with my fellow
Justice of the Peace appointees

PUBLIC SERVICE MEDAL CIRCA 1986

The Public Service Medal, or Pingat Bakti Masyarakat (PBM), is a national award instituted in 1973 to recognise meritorious contributions by citizens to the community.

Recipients of the medal are recognised for their commendable public service to Singapore, or for their achievements in the areas of arts and letters, sports, sciences, business, their professions and the labour movement.

PBM awardees are entitled to use the post-nominal letters "PBM" and also conferred the PBM silver medal. Past recipients include:-

Mr George Sandosham
Barrister and Solicitor, Singapore and Western Australia
Justice of the Peace Singapore
Former Magistrate and District Judge Singapore
Past President Tanglin Club

His wife Linda was awarded the Efficiency Medal
(Pingat Berkerbolehan) the same year George was
awarded his medal for her work at the Ministry of Education.

THE REPUBLIC OF SINGAPORE

Certificate of Appreciation

is presented to

MR GEORGE SANDOSHAM, JP, PBM

for

voluntary services as
Deputy Registrar of Marriages/Licensed Solemnizer

Dated this 11th *day of* Jan 2002

Mr Abdullah Tarmugi
Minister for Community Development and Sports, Singapore

MCD No. <u>1372</u>

THE WOMEN'S CHARTER.
(CHAPTER 353).

LICENCE TO SOLEMNIZE MARRIAGES

<table>
<tr><td>G.N. No.
S155/94</td><td>In exercise of the powers conferred by section 8 of the Women's Charter, and by virtue of the Delegation of Powers (Ministry of Community Development) Notification 1994, the Senior Minister of State, Ministry of Community Development, hereby grants   MR GEORGE SANDOSHAM, PBM a licence to solemnize marriages in Singapore, with effect from   2 April 1994</td></tr>
</table>

Dated this 6th day of April 1994.

TANG KAN HOY
REGISTRAR OF MARRIAGES, SINGAPORE
for and on behalf of the
SENIOR MINISTER OF STATE,
MINISTRY OF COMMUNITY DEVELOPMENT

"

Wives, submit to your husbands, as is fitting in the Lord. Husbands, love your wives and do not be harsh with them. Children, obey your parents in everything, for this pleases the Lord. Fathers, do not embitter your children, or they will be discouraged."

– Colossians 3:18-21 (NIV)

10

THE NEXT GENERATIONS

*Our three offspring and their families are whom we share
jovial times and memories with*

I should mention at this stage that my dad, who was as generous as I am, offered us a flat next to Gleneagles Hospital as a wedding present. Linda and I then used her savings to furnish the flat.

After a year, the first son and heir to the Sandosham fortune was born. To ensure my dad was properly thanked for the wedding gift, we named him Arthur after Dad's name – Arthur Ranadhe Sandosham ('Randi'). The godfather of my firstborn was one of my favourite uncles, who used to slip me a few dollars every time I saw him.

Arthur's birth also helped Linda's mother warm up to our marriage. Her visits gave me the opportunity to impress her with my 'virtues'. I can say with confidence that she found me a suitable son-in-law, well-earning and showering her with respect, love, and affection. I must say that she even finally agreed that Linda had made a great choice in choosing a husband and happily returned to Malaysia, after which our beloved 'Ah Soh' helped look after the children and manage our home as Linda resumed teaching and her numerous volunteer activities.

Our other two children, Paul Rabindranath Sandosham ('Rabi') and Renita Ann Sandosham ('Nita') were born in 1970 and 1974 respectively. I can't say 'raising kids is hard' as a whole – that's because Linda did much of it, especially the hard bits like punishment, reprimanding, disciplining and all the important tasks of bringing up the kids. I would say that to some extent, I participated in the raising of our children the same way that I myself was raised – in an easy-going manner, and Linda will say I was hardly the disciplinarian between us.

So, the kids and I largely kept out of each other's way, and so long as they did well and passed their exams, I was fine. I am exceedingly proud of them as none of them misbehaved or gave us any trouble. To my knowledge, they didn't drink or smoke and were overall very well-behaved kids.

They have also done well academically and adopted some measure of my influence in their lives (not through duress, I assure you!): Randi has a Masters of Law degree (although he doesn't practice it) and now lives in Singapore. Rabi is a Partner in a law firm and is also a member of the Board of Directors of The Chartered Institute of Arbitrators, previously having done litigation as I did. He resides in Singapore with his wife and daughter, who is also our only grandchild. Renita did journalism in San Francisco and worked as a journalist for a while before moving on to Human Resources. She, too, ended up with a bit of legal 'influence' in her life as she is currently a Vice President of a cloud-based electronic (legal) discovery platform. She has now settled in America.

Both Randi and Rabi became very involved in sports and rugby, which of course delighted me, and gave us all an outlet to bond. Randi played rugby for Saint Andrew's School and so did Rabi. Rabi was also a runner as I had been. The only person who didn't seem interested in sports was Nita, but she emulates (in my opinion) the foregone potential I had of being a stand-up comedian: upon graduating with a Masters in Public Administration and a basic journalism degree, she announced confidently that when Secretary of State Condoleeza Rice resigned, she would apply for her job.

I do get along pretty well with my daughter-in-law and son-in-law – I think it is because I largely don't interfere with their lives and with my son-in-law, it is easy to share a common interest in beer! The most common binding factor for us all, however, is food!

I cannot deny that Shu-En, our beloved granddaughter, is the best at bringing out my soft side. I treat her like a princess and she is thoroughly spoilt by me! All the spoiling was clearly worth it as you can see how she paid tribute to me on my 80th birthday in this eloquent poem.

When you're eighty,

You can chill out,

No worries on your mind,

No work to go to.

No sweating it out

But living it cool.

No worries about your size,

Just drink the beer of life.

And eat ice-cream every day.

You can go on and on and on and on

Until people get annoyed, ANNOYED, annoyed

You can go on holidays whenever you like

You can go on a cruise and be crazy.

You can dive into the sea and swim with the sharks

But be sure they think you are one of them

Just be happy all day long

For happiness is your name.

So be thankful you're a SANDOSHAM!

My family is a big part of my arriving at the conclusion that I have had great parents, a great wife as well as kids, and a grandchild to boot. Together with some 200 friends who I want to thank for being part of my life – I really can't complain about anything.

I am truly lucky.

MY FAMILY

Prof Sandy (my dad) cracking a joke with
Queen Elizabeth, Prince Philip & Princess Anne -
1974 at Commonwealth House, Kuala Lumpur

Surita (my niece) receiving the Queen Mother at
International Student House, London

In contrast to the privilege of my other family
members - this is my one and only photo
with the Queen

11

RETIREMENT AND MOVING TO QUEENSLAND

*'Cruising' through retirement and our (brief) sojourn in
Australia in the late 1990s*

Linda and I had originally planned to retire in Western Australia, and I was admitted to practice there in 1981. However, after retiring, I found that place too hot in summer and too cold in winter, so we moved to Gold Coast in Queensland in 1996. That was when Linda retired and we managed to get a retirement visa.

We originally applied for four years, and the next one was in 10 years. I remember the immigration officer asking me if I had any criminal record when we were applying and I was so much in love with living in Australia that I ended up asking him, "Do I need a criminal record to live here?"

I had sold our Singapore Island Country Club (SICC) membership and (as a measure of contrast in lifestyles at the time in Singapore and Australia) this procured us a four-bedroom bungalow house with a pool in Robina Woods – an area developed by Singaporean Robin Low. I had my very own mini-golf driving range in the backyard too!

I think about our move to Australia as one of the best decisions we have made to continue living life George Sandosham-style. As Linda rightly states, "those were the best years of our lives". This was largely because we found Australia an easy country in which to make friends.

Acquaintances that we met in parks became friends, and even the handymen that came over to our place to fix things were a regular drop-in. Much like Singapore, our house always had chilled beer and we made sure to offer it to anyone who walked into our home.

Truth be told, I think that is the secret to my good life and circle of friends, everywhere I went. Especially in Australia, where Aussies simply love their beer and sports. Linda came very close to becoming a representative of local women there, who admired her for her outspokenness and charming personality. We celebrated our 40th wedding anniversary there, surrounded by friends old and new, from both Singapore and Australia!

As part of our retirement, Linda and I also enjoyed taking cruises, and we indulged in this at least once a year. Our favourite was sailing on the Queen Mary 2 and we have had some great experiences on that ship!

A favourite memory of mine is sailing under the Golden Gate Bridge in San Francisco. Being a club aficionado, I could not resist drinking at the Golden Lion club (and pub). One day, a gentleman walked in with (what I assumed was) his seeing-eye or guide dog. (I assumed this because dogs are not allowed into pubs, so this must be the only reason he could enter with one.)

He had come in with another lady and sat down at a window and I was observing him. Just as the boat was passing under the bridge, I saw him take out a pair of binoculars and look through them – and he continued to pass the binoculars between himself and this lady!

I got very angry that he had come to the pub with what I thought was his guide dog, but he was clearly not blind – so I walked up to him and said, "you are supposed to be blind to be able to bring a dog in here!" He looked at me and replied, "You stupid man! My DOG is blind!"

Linda and I had many such adventures (or you could say 'misadventures'), but as I mentioned, life has a funny way of sometimes piecing itself together like a puzzle. On one voyage I noticed the Tanglin Club plaque aboard the Queen Mary 2! There was also a photo of Charlie Chaplin in his younger days and you could say the two of us certainly shared something in common!

Unfortunately, in 2017, life took another turn for the two of us when Linda was diagnosed with oral cancer. We were very lucky as the diagnosis was an early one. Linda was at one of her routine dental checkups in Australia when the dentist noticed something was not right with her gums and suggested further scans.

What followed was a diagnosis, rounds of radiation, and a fracture too! The hospital staff and doctors were kind and attentive to Linda and she took it all with gusto and confidence. She remembers me being the scared one, more so than her. I will concede and let her be right this time!

We returned to Singapore to continue Linda's treatment, which lasted for a year. It was especially hard for our children to visit us in Australia often enough, although with help from Linda's three sisters, we could manage the treatment regime. However, we then made the difficult decision to permanently move our base back to Singapore.

Thankfully, Linda is as sprightly as ever, accompanying me everywhere and continuing to put up with my shenanigans as I enjoy my one-for-one beer offer every Tuesday at the Tanglin Club. Whilst our sojourn in Australia gave us great memories, being in Singapore is not a bad life either. Whenever asked where I would rather live, I always say, *"I don't mind either country. I could fit in there; I can fit in here."*

The Castle

The backyard
driving range

On board the Queen Victoria, which we sailed
on from time to time

Club insignia on QM2

12

MY STAND ON BEER

My eternal, existential relationship with the magical brew that bridges friendships and brings good cheer

I find it appropriate at this juncture to dedicate an entire section to explaining my love affair and commitment to beer. When asked if I faced any kind of racism or bad behaviour against me while I was travelling through the world or living in Australia, my answer to it is always – "beer buys everything".

I remember on this one particular visit to London on a vacation, I entered a pub and immediately realised that all the white folks withdrew from where I was. There was a sense of unease and incomprehension, and I knew it was time to play my magic trick. I thumped a fifty-pound bill onto the bar and told the bartender, "One round of drinks for everyone here on me!" That's it – that's all it took for them to cheer and slap my back, like decades-old friends. I continued employing the same policy across my different travels and circumstances in this beer-loving world.

To further illustrate the magical powers of the brew, I have borrowed original prose by American Judge, Noah S. "Soggy" Sweat Jr, originally written about whiskey. However, I feel that my semi-plagiarised, amended version makes my beer stand truly clear:

If by beer you mean the Devil's brew,

The Poison scourge, the bloody monster that defies innocence,

Dethrones reason, creates misery and poverty, yea, literally

Takes the bread out of the mouth of the babes;

If you mean the evil drink that topples men and women from

Pinnacles of righteous, gracious living into the bottomless pit of

Despair, degradation, shame, helplessness, and hopelessness -

Then certainly I am against it with all my willpower.

But if by beer you mean the oil of conversation, the philosophic

Wine and ale that are consumed when good fellows get together,

That puts a song to their hearts, laughter on their lips

And the warm glow of contentment in their eyes;

You mean that sterling drink that puts the spring in an old

Man's steps on a frosty morning;

If you mean that drink, the sale of which pours into our

Treasury untold millions of dollars which are used to provide

Tender care for our crippled children, our pitifully aged

And infirm and to build our highways, hospitals, and schools -

Then, brother, I am for it.

This is George's stand!

13

HAPPY GEORGE

*Linda's and my social lives have, in great part, rotated around the
social clubs of Singapore, and the friends I have made there have been
a great source of happiness and joy*

The Almighty has protected me, allowing me to drink in moderation, and you have by now witnessed the central role that beer has played in life in enabling me to form my friendships and form a thriving social life. I have indeed met some very interesting characters and formed meaningful connections, with the heart of these relationships formed through club memberships.

As mentioned, I sold my membership of SICC to buy our home in Queensland, and I was also a member of the Keppel Club. However, I also sold that because we didn't end up using it with our other memberships. I am a current life member of the NUS Guild House but we are not so active there, and so our most significant memberships, friendships and community were formed at the Singapore Cricket Club (SCC) and the Tanglin Club.

Instituting the International Rugby 7s at the Singapore Cricket Club
Like every self-respecting male lawyer at the time, I joined SCC as it provided the opportunity to efficiently combine the professional with the social at a different type of 'bar' – the drinking type. I had joined SCC in September 1965, and I would have joined in 1964 but my proposer Ralph King said no blacks were allowed then as it was a white men's club. I paid S$15 to join and now it is around S$20,000!

I have great memories of drinking in the old Men's Bar at SCC. Yes, back then the SCC bar was called the "Men's Bar" and only the male variety of the human species was allowed to enter and drink there. Women were only allowed into the bar on New Year's Eve, and then they would do some wild things like jumping off the bar top. In truth, it was quite a good thing that women were not allowed – and even our wives and girlfriends agreed because they knew for sure that when we were there, we were not hanging around other women!

A thing I remember back then was a custom where they said if you had three drinks at the bar, you had to then buy a round of drinks for everybody. There was one incident when someone told me I had three drinks, but eventually found out that the third drink was just a glass of water, and not a glass of gin and tonic!

Another memory is once there was a call for Ralph King at the old Men's Bar – he was the Chairman of the Singapore Rugby 7s committee and a good friend of mine. His wife had called the bar looking for him and Ralph told the then-barman, Mr Tan, to say he was not there. Mr Tan then told his wife, "He told me to tell you he is not here"! Those were the great old days we had and I miss those friends dearly as all have passed away except for me. Perhaps, as they say, the good die young, so I am the only one left!

I met some of the most interesting guys and greatest personalities at SCC – in the sense that they all played sports, were interested in it and encouraged others to play. I joined the SCC Rugby 7s Committee and as we know, all great ideas start with drinking beer. When I found out that the guys playing it were also its organisers, a bunch of us regular imbibers sat together and and formed a new committee. I then also suggested making it an international, inter-club competition and involving our young boys. I figured our Singaporean boys would have to do National Service (NS), so rugby would be a way to help toughen them up. First, the adults would compete, then the young boys.

We were the first to approach Standard Chartered Bank, HSBC and a few other banks to contribute to setting up tents. I was given the task of getting the schoolboys to play, and for six years it became the International Rugby 7s and the Rugby World magazine referred to it as the 'swinging 7s' .

This was truly a brilliant solution as at the time, there was no professional rugby outlet in Singapore. So through this, our sons who played school rugby were also able to participate. I always had it in my mind that progressing sports in Singapore was important, and encouraging youngsters to participate was the primary and most important thing.

We ended up having some significant matches with New Zealand, Australian and English rugby teams coming to compete, as well as the Malaysian and Thai (Bangkok) clubs visiting. We had people come from overseas to play on the pitch and they were very happy, so it became an annual affair from 1981.

Rugby eventually became a significant part of SCC's sporting and social life and we even had our own box at the Hong Kong Rugby 7s, known as 'SCC T.R.H.C.M.B'! It was a token from the Hong Kong Rugby Union of whom we knew the secretary. There we were drinking big jugs of beer in our free box, while others paid hundreds or thousands of dollars to get a box!

The same guys had met in Hong Kong for the last 20 to 30 years and I miss some of the old-timers who have since passed away. Of the original committee of the 7s, there was past president Mcpherson, Ralph King, Chris Clifton, Peter Poxen, Blair Daintry and Howard Donaldson as well as myself. I want to make sure the 7s keep going.

I didn't join the SCC General Committee but I think they did a great job upgrading the club and persuading youngsters to join and use all its facilities. When I first joined, it was a very old clubhouse, with no aircon. A temporary club was built in the area where the tennis courts are until they rebuilt it. I didn't join the committee because I was persuaded to join the one at Tanglin Club instead.

Becoming President of the Tanglin Club

I joined the Tanglin Club in 1973 when they first started allowing non-white people, and my proposer was the then-President of the club – Mr John Ewing. I joined because a large number of my SCC friends were also members and it was known to be a very friendly club. I paid S$700 and now it costs S$100,000! My greatest contribution there was to become the 'first black President' – I was often referred to as 'the one who came after Nelson Mandela but before Barack Obama'.

Before becoming President, I served on most sub-committees such as Membership and Rules, the Newsletter, etc for over seven years. When I was serving on the General Committee, my job was to keep everybody happy – we had very few disputes and they were resolved quickly and quietly. I also encouraged all the committee members to use the club actively so that they could provide feedback and get to know the members we were serving.

Once I became President, as mentioned earlier, I had the privilege of admitting Singapore's President Wee Kim Wee and Prime Minister Goh Chok Tong as honorary members. I also instated the first time capsule on behalf of the club.

This will go without saying for those who know me but my favourite place at Tanglin Club is the Tavern Bar. I have a lot of memories there as I used to go about five times a week during the 1970s and 1980s. At that time, the bar extended all the way around the corner and it had a huge bell. Now there is a gong on the other side of the bar. Members used to congregate there on a regular basis and it was a place you could have drinks with friends – just like a local pub in England – before you headed home for the evening.

I enjoyed meeting with my regular friends (there were over twelve of us). We would normally show up after work and maybe after drinks at the SCC (many of my friends were members of both clubs as I was). A lot of club committee members were part of this regular group, and we really had a good time and became very close. Their companionship is a great memory of mine and I have stayed lifelong friends with many until they passed away.

Back then, we had a much larger population of expats at the club – there could only be a maximum of 4000 to 5000 members, and only ever 51 percent of any one nationality.

As such, it was a great international club. We would all drink beer together and talk about sports and politics, and I enjoyed socialising with many cultures and attending numerous functions in the Churchill room from Christmas and New Year's Eve to St George's Day and St Andrew's Day.

We had a lot of foreign entertainers as well. I once met Max Bygraves – a famous singer from the United Kingdom who often performed in the Churchill room.

Celebrities were also not an uncommon sight. One of the foremost 'World Number One' celebrities I had the pleasure of meeting whilst I was President was the famous golfer Mr Greg Norman. As there was no golf course at Tanglin, we played at the Tanah Merah Golf Club during a Johnny Walker-sponsored event. Being a sportsman, I was convinced that my golf was actually quite 'on par' until Mr Norman told me quite unequivocally during the game to stick to my day job!

I also had the pleasure of encountering rugby legend Sir Colin Meads (the first New Zealand All Blacks player to ever be knighted), and Sean Fitzpatrick, the New Zealand rugby team All Blacks captain at the time. Being a lifelong rugby fan, these meetings have been one of the highlights of my life.

I really hope that the Tanglin Club culture stays strong. It is a 'well behaved' club where members respect each other, the staff are excellent and very loyal, long-term employees. I have seen it grow in size and stature – for instance, the pool is much larger now and all of the rooms, as well as the squash and tennis courts, were not there previously. It would be nice if its atmosphere of friendliness and camaraderie is maintained, and it stays one of the top social clubs in Singapore and beyond.

As a Life Member, I still visit the Tavern Bar every Tuesday for my one-for-one Tiger Beer deals. There are still some regulars I meet to drink with, but in truth, there are not many of us left. You should come and join me there! I'll buy you a beer.

With the president
of the SCC

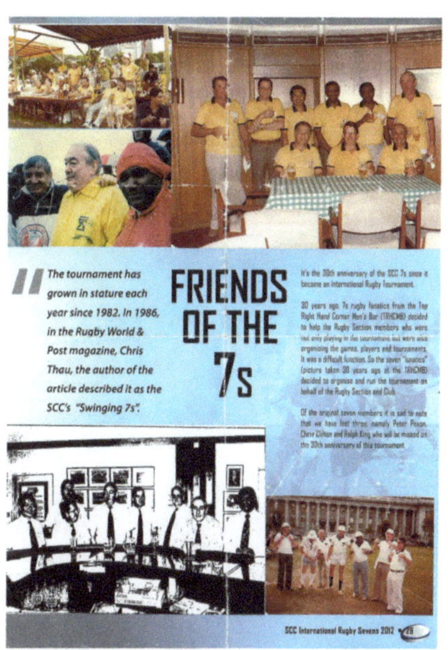

Swinging 7s'
(extract from SCC magazine)

The SCC 7s committee

Our SCC 7s box in
Hong Kong

The plaque of past presidents at the
Tanglin Club (currently on display)

With past presidents of the
Tanglin Club

Laying the first time capsule at
the Tanglin Club (extract from
the Tanglin Club magazine)

Myself and Linda at a
Tanglin Club event

Photo with Mr Max Bygraves

Playing golf with
Mr Greg Norman

Photo with
Mr Sean Fitzpatrick

Photo of the Life Members
plaque at the Tanglin Club

Photo with Mr Colin Meads

"

Two things I ask of you, Lord;

do not refuse me before I die:

Keep falsehood and lies far from me;

give me neither poverty nor riches,

but give me only my daily bread."

– Proverbs 30:7-8 (NIV)

14

EPILOGUE

When I am asked if I have any regrets in life, I can, without a shadow of a doubt, say – none! I have lived a happy, content (albeit boring) life, and hold no grudges or wishes. I have experienced lifelong friendships, an interesting career, spent the best time with my dear wife and children, travelled the world, and had the good fortune of finding beer wherever I went.

As I mentioned earlier – a great many people have had an impact on and influenced my life. Though many have come and gone – I would nonetheless like to acknowledge their role and contribution to my life as they have all left me with happy memories. This is by no means an exhaustive list but I could narrate a short history about each and every one of them because they are men I have admired, adored, or respected for their generosity, compassion and appreciation shown to me in my 84 years on this planet. (My immediate family is excluded for obvious reasons and I express my deepest apologies to any friend whose name I may have inadvertently omitted – I hope I will be eventually forgiven!).

A true friend is the greatest blessing, and as you get older friends may decrease in size but increase in value.

A. Neysadurai

Alan Thambiayah

Alan Whitehead

Dr Alex Delilkan

Alistair Izat

Alistair MacPherson

Amarjit Singh

Andre Ruyters

Andrew Kefford

Andrew Phang

Anwarul Haque

Asoka Uduwela

Barry Annabel

Ben Dudley

Bez Kekesi

Bill Cutts

Bill Gartshore

Dr Bill Hoyer

Blair Daintry

Bradley Boyd

Brian MacDonald

Brian Verity

Bryan Selvaratnam

Chandra Mohan

Dr Chan Onn Leng

Justice Chan Sek Keong

Charlie Phua

Dr Chiang Hai Ding

Dato Chiem Chong Woo

Chin Yee

Chris Clifton

Chris Shadforth

Chris Teo

Choo Teck Long

Chung Seng Ghee

Claude Oliveiro

Clive Fairfield

Dave Kuipers

Dave Parry

Dave Wogan

David Hodge

David Hor

David James

David Kraal

David Murphy

Dennis D'Cotta

Des Coleman

Dr Dhanwant Singh

Don Gallop

Donny James

Ebert Alwis

Ed McGivern

Edward D'Souza

Edward Seow

Ernest Devadason

Errol Foenander

Eugene Hor

Eugene Tan

Francis Lim

Francis Remedios

Freddy Vias

Gavin Salt

George Paul

Giam Chin Toon

Glen Sheares

Goh Chok Tong

Dr Gopal Baratham

Graham Packett

Graham Reardon

Greg Kee

Col Gucharan Singh

Gurdip Singh

Haider Sithawalla

Hamish Christie

Harry Blackburn

Henry Hockstadt

Herman Hockstadt

Horace Langlois

Howard Donaldson

Howard Henshaw

Hugh Cave

Ian Booth

Ian Chambers

Ian Faulkner

Ivan Allan

Jacob Puthenparambil

James Pandian

Jared Thum

Jesse Chevrez

Jim Alston

Jim Chadwick

Dr Jimmy How

Jimmy Lee

Jimmy Mendrick

Joe Grimberg

John Bailey

John Blair

John Clark

John Ewing

John Sheridan

John Thomson

John Vias

Johnny Ong

KT Alexander

Ken Whiting

Kenneth Ho

Prof Kenny Ong

Koh Poh Tiong

K. Kulasegaram

Lawrence Chan

Laurie Poots

Lee Pope

Dr Leo Taylor

Len Foster

Dr Lim Lean Huat

Lim Ng Koo

Lim Say Chong

Dr Lim Say Wan

Dr Lindy Lin

Dr Lionel Rasanayagam

Low Sin Cheok

MK Sen

M Puvanendran

Malcom Fleming

Malcom Smithson

Manu Bhogwani

Mario Rousch

Micheal Cheok

Micheal Khoo

Mike Sharpe

Mike Yeoman

Prof Mulkit Singh

N Ganesan

Nicholas Ong

Nick Yacoeal

Norman D'Souza

Norman Jones

Ong Kee Jin

P.Coomaraswamy

Padbiri

Paddy Donoghue Jr

Dato Parakash

Pat Donoghue

Pat Paulo

Patrick Gower

Paul Lawless

Paul Miller

Peter Ashforth

Peter Oei

Peter Poxon

Peter Sayers

Peter Tomkins

Phang Ngit Min

Phil Shepard

Philip Seow

Rabi Doraisamy

Rajan Menon

Ralph King

Col Rankin

Ram Naidu

Ravi Pannell

Ray Lynch

Ray Serpent

Dr Raymond Lopes

Reggie Da Silva

Reggie Thein

Richard Hall

Richard Magness

Richard Pannell

Dato Robert Chiem

Robin Tessensohn

Rubin H Mohideen

Russell Koh

S Sinnappa

S Rajendran

S.Sangkaran

Prof SS Ratnam

ST Ratnam

Shapy Khan

Dr B R Sreenivasan

Steven Tai

Stewart Mole

Sydney Oliveiro

Syed Alwee Alsree

Dr T I Williams

T P B Menon

Justice T Sinnathuray

T T Goei

T.Tiruchelvarayan

Tan Bak Choon

Tan Cheng Guan

Tauler Sandosham

Tay Soo Tee

Ted De Ponti

Ted Grinsted

Ted Wilson

Thomas Hoi

Tong Yew Sum

Dr Ung Eng Lim

Victor Choo

Von Lueckenhausen

President Wee Kim Wee

William Fonseka

Dr Winston Koh

Yelle De Vries

Yeoh En Lai

As I complete 84 years on this planet, I am therefore reminded every day of the great fortune to have travelled and lived a life filled with adventures and experiences – one that makes me want to go back and live it all again.

Would I want to change anything?

No, not a thing.

15

AFTERWORD(S)

When you've been married to someone for as long as 56 years, you become as the proverbial saying goes 'two peas in a pod'. This is the most apt description I can think of regarding my married life to George.

Of course with his 'weird' sense of humour – he likes to describe our 56 years together as 'a lifetime of penal servitude' – but I have no doubt that among our family and friends, most will neither take his words seriously nor empathise with him.

What I wish to say is that the George I know is exactly the George known to his family and friends. Like him or not – he remains true to himself, and anything I say will be no more revealing than what we already know of him.

My deepest respect for him comes from knowing that – because while we have had many a confrontation throughout the years, and of widely differing things, we have always found a solution (amicable or otherwise) to resolve issues.

This has been done unconditionally and living by the pure and simple truth 'forgive and let live'. However, more importantly, despite being like two peas in a pod for ever so long, I am most thankful that we can each be our own persons – two different individuals. I have always been able to pursue my own passions and interests in my marriage to George, as has he, and for this I am ever grateful and thankful that we have always given each other the respect and the 'space' to truly 'be ourselves'.

Linda Sandosham

The title of the book is very apt as Pops is indeed one lucky fellow, blessed with good fortune. He has had a relatively peaceful and relaxing life due to his laidback and easy-going demeanour. He has been a good father who loves and cares for all his children and has provided well for us in our growing years.

One early recollection I have of him is sitting in his big armchair eating and watching television. Though he might not be one to display affection, he does it in his own way by dishing out praises and being his generous self in doling out cash – for this I have always been grateful!

Another thing that will always stick in my mind is Pops holding a beer as evidenced from all the photos he is in. Beer (usually Tiger beer) and Pops go hand-in-hand to the extent that it might be surmised he is actually their poster boy and should perhaps be remunerated as he promotes it wherever he goes!

Pops is a popular guy judging from the many friends and acquaintances he has made over the years – many of whom have told me how much of a great guy he is, notwithstanding his shortcomings. He seems to have accumulated a 'United Nations' of friends spanning the globe encompassing family friends made here in Singapore to expatriate friends befriended at his second and third 'homes' (namely the Tanglin Club and Singapore Cricket Club) to ones made during his travels.

What amazes and surprises me are the age gaps as some are half his age or even younger! I figure a lot has to do with his charming and friendly persona, as well as his ability to spin tales of his past life as a magistrate and lawyer, tell corny jokes and make pronouncements with favourite lines like "Don't be a cheap carpet" and "It's just not cricket!" Revelling in the limelight, he once did an impersonation of Stevie Wonder complete with sunglasses when he lived on the Gold Coast – I can say he certainly lapped up the adulation he got from that!

Even all of Mom's relatives, both young and old, are very fond of him and comprise part of the 'posse' of followers he seems to have amassed over the years to serve him hand and foot. Besides Mom (and of course myself), the list of his other 'subjects' include Ah Soh (our housekeeper), Auntie Jane (his 'personal cook'), Mom's sisters Winnie, Lana and Queenie (though Lana would draw the line at getting him a glass of water), Chauffeur Hamdi, Office Manager Lim, Secretary Linda and his 'partner in crime' Gurdip Singh. No doubt there are many others who have been inadvertently co-opted!

Notwithstanding Pops' diet of beer, curries, local delights, desserts and ice-creams, he has been blessed with good genes and long life (both my grandparents had a long life free of major health problems). On one rare occasion, a doctor who examined him was dumbfounded and arrived at the conclusion he is a medical miracle given his age, physique and indolent lifestyle. He will attest that his secret is that he has no stress and sleeps 14 hours a day. (Little does he know that the stress has been passed on to those around him).

Most of all, Pops has been blessed with Mom who faithfully and steadfastly stood by him all these years and put up with his vices and shortcomings. As much as he attributes much of his success to himself, which is true to a certain degree, he does acknowledge he would not be living such a comfortable and easy life without Mom, with the addition of myself and my siblings not being 'a thorn in his side'.

He often reminds us that had he not had to provide for us, he would not have been 'poverty-stricken' and for that we owe him big time – I couldn't ask for more in a father like him!

Arthur Sandosham

Those who know my father will know that he is a man of simple needs. If you took the time to break it down, he has only two simple pleasures – a freshly poured cold pint of Tiger draft beer and the company of his friends. Apart from his ten hours of beauty sleep each evening, he needs nothing else as while friends and family would often fret over gifts to give him for Christmas (ranging from socks to pyjamas to underwear) – it soon became apparent to me that the only present he truly treasured were the two cases of Tiger Beer he would receive from his dear friend Koh Poh Tiong every Christmas Day. Without fail, both cases would be promptly consumed by my father between Christmas and New Year.

His love for the golden ale and drinking buddies is amply demonstrated by the fact that much of my childhood was spent waiting for him to finish his "one for the road" pint at the Men's Bar of the Singapore Cricket Club (specifically, The Right Hand Corner Men's Bar) and the Tanglin Club. He would hold court in the company of his many friends, regaling them with stories of his life as a public prosecutor, district judge and criminal defence lawyer.

Apart from his time at these social clubs, he would often invite random friends over to his own bar at home at Redwood Avenue, Kingsmead Road and Balmoral Park, where the home fridge was always well stocked with cold beers. House parties were a common occurrence growing up. Apart from the Annual Sandosham Open House where several hundred people would appear on Christmas Day for a day of feasting and drinking, there were parties held to celebrate a multitude of events including birthdays, wedding anniversaries, FA Cup Finals, Wimbledon etc.

I soon figured out these were merely excuses to allow my father to invite friends over and consume copious amounts of alcohol; retirement and moving to the Gold Coast did not change things a bit. He continued to be the centre of attraction and entertainment at the Robina Tavern, where he was fondly known as 'The Hanging Judge'. While patience isn't his finest virtue, it is fair to say that he never had a harsh word to say about anyone, except of course the barman who took too long to refill his empty beer mug.

As he reaches his 84th year and as the title of this book will attest, my father has been blessed with good fortune. Not financial fortune or great fame – but something even better than that. He was indeed fortunate to meet and be married to Mom, who for the best part of 56 years, has supported and tolerated him.

Paul Sandosham

I've been told several times over the years that I'm my father's daughter, which one can only hope was meant as a compliment. In any case I'll choose to take it as such, as I optimistically believe I have inherited his enormous sense of humour which is sometimes self-deprecating and often wickedly snarky. I also have his giant appetite for socialising (but only if you're interesting – and let's face it, most people rarely are). We also share a similar zest for indulging in the finer things in life (preferably if someone else is picking up the tab).

While I don't remember Pops helping me with my homework or other mundane aspects of my school years, I received plenty of life lessons at the bar that have formed the foundation for how I network, negotiate, and advocate for myself.

As the world we live in hardens into increasingly partisan divides among the righteous and the self-righteous, I am forever grateful for having a father who never took anything too seriously and who believed common ground could always be found after sharing a few beers.

Renita Sandosham

What I admire most about Uncle Suku (as I call my uncle George and is the affectionate family name for him used in our family) – is that he is such an optimist. This optimism bolsters his natural ability to be funny and canny about various goings-on, whether at the Singapore Bar or the local watering holes he loves to frequent. He is the embodiment of the hail-fellow-well-met character and is a magnet for similar beings seeking such joy.

My uncle reminds me most of his father, who also had much to be proud of, and was as famous for his off-colour jokes as he was for eradicating malaria. I will always remember my grandfather reminding me that his success was due to my grandmother by quoting that "behind every successful man is a successful wife" and that is also true for Uncle Suku. He is a man of substance because of my loving aunt Linda, and I expect that is why if there was a favourite son, it was always my Uncle Suku. He epitomises all that is to be a Sandosham – which, after all, means 'happiness' in Tamil.

Surita Sandosham (George's niece).

16

DEDICATION

This 'captivating' story is dedicated to:

My Mom and Dad who gave me everything from birth

My brother Reggie and sister Sujatha who protected me

My wife of fifty-six years, Linda, for having looked after me from the day of marriage

My three children, Randi, Rabi and Renita for giving me an easy fatherhood

My one and only grandchild Shu-En for giving me the joy of grandparenthood

My son-in-law, Brad, my daughter-in-law, Candace, and Gloria for their kindness and affection toward me

Last but not least, to scores of friends and relatives who have been kind to me and given me a full and happy life.

A special thank you goes to Jacob Puthenparambil for his interest and help in doing this book. My thanks also go to Shirani Alfreds and Mariyam Haider for doing much of the work in bringing the story of my life to fruition.

REFERENCES

'$124,000 Payroll Grab: Man Charged with Murder of PUB Driver', The Straits Times, 22 September 1970,
https://eresources.nlb.gov.sg/newspapers/Digitised/Article/straitstimes19700922-1.2.60.

'6 Months' Jail for Two Found Guilty of Outraging Girl's Modesty', The Straits Times, 5 December 1969,
https://eresources.nlb.gov.sg/newspapers/Digitised/Article/straitstimes19691205-1.2.73.

'57 Pass Final Examination for Bachelor of Law', The Straits Times, 25 February 1965,
https://eresources.nlb.gov.sg/newspapers/Digitised/Article/straitstimes19650225-1.2.105.

'Asthmatic Cashier Gets Traffic Charge Acquittal', The Straits Times, 25 March 1971,
https://eresources.nlb.gov.sg/newspapers/Digitised/Article/straitstimes19710325-1.2.89.

'Bar Admission', Straits Budget, 23 March 1966,
https://eresources.nlb.gov.sg/newspapers/Digitised/Article/straitsbudget19660323-1.2.61.

'Caning Order of Six Strokes Is Lifted', The Straits Times, 30 April 1980,
https://eresources.nlb.gov.sg/newspapers/Digitised/Article/straitstimes19800430-1.2.65.

'DAY ONE AND THE FIRST SIX WEEKS' (SAFTI Military Institute), accessed 12 May 2022,
https://www.mindef.gov.sg/oms/safti/one-of-kind-2nd-ed2015/chp/011_day1-1st-6wks.pdf.

'Hai Yuen Soars to Heights Anew', The Singapore Free Press, 3 August 1954,
https://eresources.nlb.gov.sg/newspapers/Digitised/Article/freepress19540803-1.2.107.

'Jail Term Set aside after Appeal to Give Youth Another Chance', The Straits Times, 11 November 1972,
https://eresources.nlb.gov.sg/newspapers/Digitised/Article/straitstimes19721111-1.2.35.

'Jesse's Last Words To Youth "Serve Your Fellowmen"', Singapore Standard, 11 November 1955, Newspaper SG - eresources.

'Lawyer Pleads Guilty...', New Nation, 24 October 1972,
https://eresources.nlb.gov.sg/newspapers/Digitised/Article/newnation19721024-1.2.12.

'Letters', The Straits Times, 20 June 1960,
https://eresources.nlb.gov.sg/newspapers/Digitised/Article/straitstimes19600620-1.2.50.1.

'MEET SINGAPORE'S FUTURE CHAMPIONS', The Singapore Free Press, 13 April 1957,
https://eresources.nlb.gov.sg/newspapers/Digitised/Article/freepress19570413-1.2.62.

'MissX Is Asked about Her First "Affair"', The Straits Times, 29 June 1973,
https://eresources.nlb.gov.sg/newspapers/Digitised/Article/straitstimes19730629-1.2.68.

'Motorist Prefers to Be Jailed', The Straits Times, 9 February 1971,
https://eresources.nlb.gov.sg/newspapers/Digitised/Article/straitstimes19710209-1.2.87.

'One for Hubby and Another for Me', The Straits Times, 10 August 1986,
https://eresources.nlb.gov.sg/newspapers/Digitised/Article/straitstimes19860810-1.2.17.3.

'Pereira Case Is Heard behind Closed Doors', The Straits Times, 27 November 1970,
https://eresources.nlb.gov.sg/newspapers/Digitised/Article/straitstimes19701127-1.2.74.

'Portrait of Messrs. Len Foster and George Sandosham', accessed 11 April 2022,
https://eresources.nlb.gov.sg/printheritage/image.aspx?id=c5b19e73-4127-43a5-ba82-
51556b148e68.

'PRESIDENT ONG TENG CHEONG PRESIDING AT THE APPOINTMENT CEREMONY OF
JUSTICES OF THE PEACE AT THE ISTANA', 1 March 1994,
https://www.nas.gov.sg/archivesonline/photographs/record-details/114d647c-1162-11e3-
83d5-0050568939ad.

'R.I. Juniors Win', The Straits Times, 26 November 1953,
https://eresources.nlb.gov.sg/newspapers/Digitised/Article/straitstimes19531126-1.2.186.

'Rugby Fiesta May Rival HK Tourney', Singapore Monitor, 2nd Edition, 24
February 1983, https://eresources.nlb.gov.sg/newspapers/Digitised/Article/
singmonitor19830224-2.2.35.6.

'Sandosham Gets a Top WHO Post in Manila', The Straits Times, 28 May 1960,
https://eresources.nlb.gov.sg/newspapers/Digitised/Article/straitstimes19600528-1.2.51.

'Sandosham Resigns', New Nation, 2 June 1971,
https://eresources.nlb.gov.sg/newspapers/Digitised/Article/newnation19710602-1.2.17.

'SANDOSHAM WAS BEST OF RECORD-BREAKERS', The Straits Times, 26 June 1955,
https://eresources.nlb.gov.sg/newspapers/Digitised/Article/straitstimes19550626-1.2.140.

'Shooting Case: Court Urged to Amend Charge', The Straits Times, 26 March 1976,
https://eresources.nlb.gov.sg/newspapers/Digitised/Article/straitstimes19760326-1.2.74.

'STORE JUDGE TO ENTER PRIVATE PRACTICE', The Straits Times, 16 May 1970,
https://eresources.nlb.gov.sg/newspapers/Digitised/Article/straitstimes19700516-1.2.104.

'Two Are Sworn in as New Magistrates', The Straits Times, 26 April 1966,
https://eresources.nlb.gov.sg/newspapers/Digitised/Article/straitstimes19660426-1.2.40.

'UNIVERSITY 1-1', The Straits Times, 12 March 1963,
https://eresources.nlb.gov.sg/newspapers/Digitised/Article/straitstimes19630312-1.2.95.

'Varsity Miss Martens and Give Army First Win', The Singapore Free Press, 15 May 1961,
https://eresources.nlb.gov.sg/newspapers/Digitised/Article/freepress19610515-1.2.101.

Redhill Publishing

Redhill Publishing is the publishing arm of Redhill – a responsive, agile and full-service global communications firm. The company provides strategic counsel for public relations, digital narratives, crisis management, internal communications, content & research, design, web & video development and branding across industries and sectors. Driven by a team of passionate communications specialists, Redhill crafts campaigns that build a brand's reputation and market share.

Headquartered in Singapore and embedded in Southeast Asia, with a reach that extends to North and South Asia, Australia, the Middle East, Europe and the US, Redhill's close-knit, multi-national team of communications specialists and public relations consultants work to support our clients across the globe.

Redhill is recognised as one of Singapore's Fastest Growing Companies by Statista and The Straits Times (2022), Financial Times' top 500 Asia-Pacific High-Growth Companies (2021) and is the first public relations agency to be recognised in the Enterprise 50 Awards (2020).